Picture the Past
Life on the
OREGON TRAIL

Sally Senzell Isaacs

Heinemann Library
Chicago, Illinois

© 2000 Heinemann Library,
an imprint of Capstone Global Library,LLC
Chicago, IL

Customer Service 888-454-2279

Visit our website at www.heinemannlibrary.com

Produced for Heinemann Library by Bender Richardson
White.
Editor: Lionel Bender
Designer: Ben White
Picture Researcher: Cathy Stastny
Media Conversion and Typesetting: MW Graphics
Production Controller: Kim Richardson

11
11

Printed in China by Leo Paper Products Ltd

Library of Congress Cataloging-in-Publication Data.
Isaacs, Sally Senzell, 1950–
    Life on the Oregon Trail / Sally Senzell Isaacs.
        p. cm.   (Picture the past)
    Includes bibliographical references and index.
Summary: An introduction to what life was like on the
Oregon Trail, describing the wagons, daily routines, food,
clothing, Native Americans encountered on the way, and
dangers.

ISBN 1-57572-317-4 (lib. bdg.) 1-58810-302-1 (pbk.)
ISBN 978-1-57572-317-4(HC)   ISBN 978-1-58810-302-4(pbk)
1. Pioneers-Oregon Trail-History-Juvenile literature. 2.
Pioneers- Oregon Trail--Social life and customs-Juvenile
literature. 3. Frontier and pioneer life-Oregon Trail-Juvenile
literature. 4. Overland journeys to the Pacific-Juvenile
literature. 5. Oregon Trail-History-Juvenile literature. (1.
Frontier and pioneer life-Oregon Trail. 2. Overland
journeys to the Pacific. 3. Oregon Trail.) I. Title.
F597 .177 2000
978' .02-dc21   00-020645

Special thanks to Mike Carpenter, Scott Westerfield, and
Tristan Boyer-Binns at Heinemann Library for editorial and
design guidance and direction.

Acknowledgments
The producers and publishers are grateful to the
following for permission to reproduce copyright material:
Corbis: Phil Scheimeister, p. 11; Layne Kennedy, p. 12;
Michael Lewis, p. 23; James L. Amos, p. 24; Peter Newark's
American Pictures, pp. 3. 6, 10, 13, 14, 15, 17, 18, 19, 25, 28,
29; North Wind Pictures, pp. 1, 7, 8, 9, 16, 20, 21, 26.

Cover photograph: Peter Newark's American Pictures

Illustrations by John James, p. 22; James Field, 4, 29;
Gerald Wood, p. 13.
Maps by Stefan Chabluk
Cover make-up by Mike Pilley, Pelican Graphics.

Note the the Reader
Some words are shown in bold, **like this**.
You can find out what they mean by looking in the
glossary.

ABOUT THIS BOOK

This book tells about daily life of
the families who traveled on the
Oregon Trail from 1840 to 1880.
The Oregon Trail led from
Missouri to Oregon Country,
which included today's states of
Washington, Oregon, and Idaho,
parts of Montana and Wyoming,
and part of Canada. The people
headed west to find free land.
We have illustrated the book with
paintings and photographs from
this time and with artists' ideas of
how things looked then. We have
also included some modern
photographs of people dressed as
pioneers and of wagons that
remain from Oregon Trail times.

The Consultant
Diane Smolinski has years of experience
interpreting standards documents and
putting them into practice in fourth and
fifth grade classrooms.

The Author
Sally Senzell Isaacs is a professional writer
and editor of nonfiction books for children.
She graduated from Indiana University,
earning a B.S. degree in Education with
majors in American History and Sociology.
For some years, she was the Editorial
Director of Reader's Digest Educational
Division. Sally Senzell Isaacs lives in New
Jersey with her husband and two children.

CONTENTS

A Long Journey West

Before 1840, most Americans lived east of the Mississippi River. They lived on farms or in towns. Some brave explorers traveled west. They brought back stories of wide-open, free land. They also told of the Native Americans who had been living on the land for many, many years.

In the 1840's, thousands of people traveled the Oregon Trail to Oregon. These **pioneers** left friends and homes behind them. They spent four to six months walking across America.

Look for these
The illustration of a boy and girl traveler shows you the subject of each double-page story in the book.

The illustration of a wagon highlights panels with facts and figures about everyday life on the Oregon Trail.

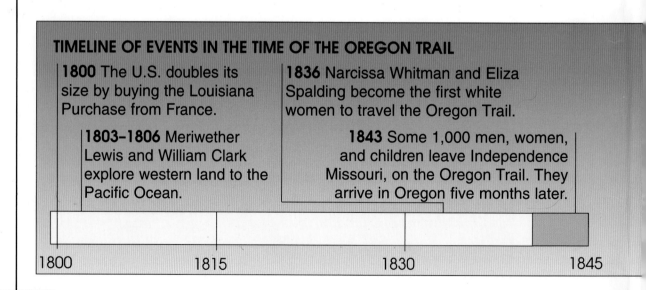

TIMELINE OF EVENTS IN THE TIME OF THE OREGON TRAIL

1800 The U.S. doubles its size by buying the Louisiana Purchase from France.

1803–1806 Meriwether Lewis and William Clark explore western land to the Pacific Ocean.

1836 Narcissa Whitman and Eliza Spalding become the first white women to travel the Oregon Trail.

1843 Some 1,000 men, women, and children leave Independence Missouri, on the Oregon Trail. They arrive in Oregon five months later.

1800   1815   1830   1845

The Oregon Trail started in Independence, Missouri. It was 2,000 miles (3,200 kilometers) long. Families came there from many places. They wanted to travel in large groups. Some people split off the Oregon Trail at the Snake River and took the California Trail to Sacramento, California.

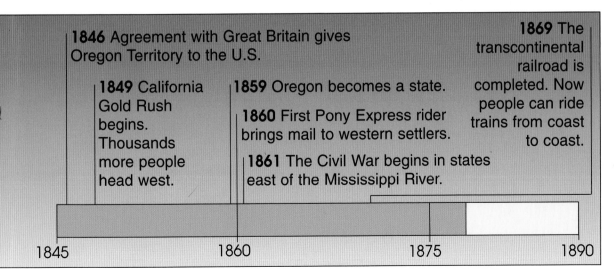

1846 Agreement with Great Britain gives Oregon Territory to the U.S.

1849 California Gold Rush begins. Thousands more people head west.

1859 Oregon becomes a state.

1860 First Pony Express rider brings mail to western settlers.

1861 The Civil War begins in states east of the Mississippi River.

1869 The transcontinental railroad is completed. Now people can ride trains from coast to coast.

| 1845 | 1860 | 1875 | 1890 |

Leaving Home

Every May, the town of Independence in Missouri was filled with excitement and tears. Dozens of families came from towns far and near. They each brought a wagon filled with their most important belongings and with cooking equipment to use on the trail. Everyone had said goodbye to relatives, friends, teachers, and homes.

The early part of the Oregon Trail crossed flat **plains**. It was too dangerous to travel the trail alone. People joined together in a **wagon train**.

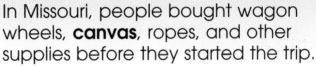

In Missouri, people bought wagon wheels, **canvas**, ropes, and other supplies before they started the trip.

These families were joining a wagon train to Oregon Country. They all had dreams of getting free land, building new homes, and starting new farms. They gave up almost everything to follow this dream.

The trip was long and hard. On the Oregon Trail, the families had to drive their wagons across plains and rivers and over the **Rocky Mountains**.

The Wagon

Strong **oxen** pulled the wooden wagons. A wagon was a little smaller than today's mini-van. The sides were about 3 feet (1 meter) high. A white **canvas** cloth covered the wagon. The cloth kept out the wind and rain.

WHAT TO TAKE

FOR THE TRIP: Water buckets, ropes, canvas, food, lantern, blankets, pans, rifles, tents, pen and paper.
FOR THE NEW HOME: Tools, seeds, spinning wheel, family photographs.

Families also brought cows for milk, chickens for eggs, and sheep for wool. Some also brought horses to ride on.

Today, visitors at Scotts Bluff, Nebraska, can see this copy of a wagon on the Oregon Trail.

The wagon was fully loaded with belongings. There was little room for people to ride inside. Sometimes a sick person or a grandparent sat in the wagon. Sometimes mothers with babies rode inside. A few people rode on horseback. Everyone else walked.

Following the Trail

Hundreds of years ago, Native Americans traveled over parts of the Oregon Trail. Their feet wore paths along rivers and between mountains. The first White **pioneers** could hardly see these paths. After a few years, wagon wheels made the trail wider and easier to follow.

The Oregon Trail crossed rivers and steep mountains. It also ran through land where Native Americans lived.

Travelers started the trip in May when there was plenty of fresh spring grass for the animals to eat. Travelers who started late faced great danger. Snowstorms hit the **Rocky Mountains** in October. Everyone had to cross the mountains before it snowed.

Passing pioneers carved their names and the date on rocks along the trail. This helped others to find their way.

The Daily Routine

The **wagon train** stopped every night for the **pioneers** and animals to eat and rest. At 4:00 in the morning, someone blew a bugle. It was time to wake up. Women started a campfire and cooked breakfast. Children rounded up the animals and milked the cows. Men took down the tents and checked the wagons.

SUNRISE TO SUNSET

4:00 A.M. Wake up and eat breakfast
7:00 A.M. Start moving along the trail
12:00 NOON Eat lunch and feed the animals
6:00 P.M. Stop for the night and make a campfire

Travelers looked for landmarks, like Chimney Rock in Nebraska, to know how far they had traveled.

Some days were boring. For eleven hours, the wagons rolled over dusty, flat **plains**. But there were plenty of exciting days. When the wagons reached a deep stream, the **oxen** became scared. The people had to pull the animals through the water. They floated the wagons. Everyone swam across.

The front wagons kicked up lots of dust. Every family wanted their wagon in the front so they would not have to breathe the dust. Usually people took turns in front.

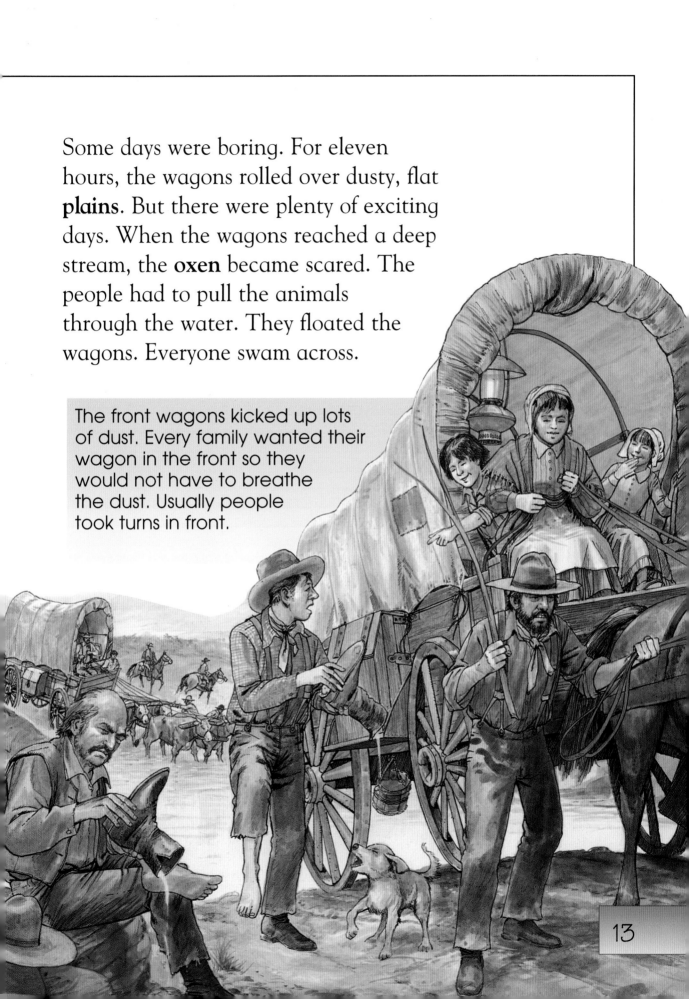

Night on the Trail

As soon as the wagons stopped, boys helped their fathers fix broken wheels and take care of the animals. Girls helped their mothers cook supper and mend clothes. Some men and boys took turns to stay awake by the campfire. They were **guards** against wild animals and Native Americans who tried to steal the animals.

Towards the end of the day, **guides** rode ahead of the **wagon train** to find a good place to stop for the night.

At night, the travelers formed a circle with their wagons. People felt safe to see everyone around them.

Usually each family ate by their own wagon. Sometimes families got together by a campfire to share stories, play music, or celebrate a birthday. Most people slept in tents. Some slept inside the wagon on top of boxes.

Children on the Trail

Children had responsibilities such as helping their parents, watching younger brothers and sisters, and looking after animals.

As the wagons rolled along, children ran up and down the trail. They played games with friends. They picked wild flowers to make necklaces. They peered across the **plains** to search for **prairie dog** towns and buffalo herds.

Parents brought books and **slates** in the wagon. Some children practiced reading and writing every day. All children learned special lessons never taught in school. They learned how to listen for the sound of a rattlesnake. They learned to tell a coyote's call from a wolf's howl.

At lunchtime stops, the children released the **oxen** and joined with family and friends. Most families had three or four children.

HOW WOULD YOU FEEL?

Some children loved camping out every night and waking up to new adventures. Other children did not like living with strange people and sights. For some, the quiet nights were scary.

Native Americans

The Oregon Trail ran right through Native American land. Native Americans had lived on this land for thousands of years. The **wagon trains** looked frightening to them. The **pioneers** were also afraid of the Native Americans.

Sometimes Native Americans attacked the wagon trains. They were trying to protect their land.

The Native Americans closely watched the pioneers. Sometimes they showed the pioneers hidden paths across the **Rocky Mountains**.

Most Native Americans were helpful. They used their boats to take pioneers across rivers. They helped the travelers find food. However, from the 1850s onward, some pioneers stayed at places along the Oregon Trail and built homes and fences on the land. The United States government made the Native Americans leave.

FAIR TRADING

Here are some things that were **traded** between Native Americans and pioneers.

NATIVE AMERICAN THINGS
- Buffalo skins
- Fresh meat
- Smoked fish

PIONEER THINGS
- Wool blankets
- Smoked fish
- Sewing needles
- Pancakes

Dangers

Pioneers faced dangerous weather all along the trip. Thunderstorms swept across the **plains**. Then came the hot, dry desert with its swarming flies. Most of all, the pioneers feared a snowstorm in the mountains. That is why they hurried to get through the mountains before winter.

Snowstorms were deadly. Pioneers lost the trails. With no grass to eat, many animals died.

Mountain trails were narrow and rocky. Often, wagon wheels hit a rock and could not be fixed. Travelers had to continue their trip with no wagon. Their friends shared their supplies with them.

It was very hard to get the wagons over the mountains. In some jagged places, the travelers pulled the wagons up with ropes. They lowered them, inch by inch, on the other side. Some people had to empty their wagons and take them apart. They carried the pieces and their belongings across the mountains, then rebuilt the wagons.

TRAIL GRAVES

Many travelers got sick. Some got well but others died. Their friends and family buried them by the trail.

Fort Laramie

Native Americans met **fur traders** at Fort Laramie. They traded animal skins for guns, traps, and food.

After walking for seven weeks, the travelers reached Fort Laramie, Wyoming. There they found supply stores, offices, and a place to rest for a few days. Native Americans lived outside the **fort**. They came to **trade** with the travelers.

This store sold pots, pans, food, and tools to repairs wagon wheels.

PASSING THROUGH

When they arrived at Fort Laramie, travelers signed a book. That book showed that 9,000 wagons—with 40,000 men, women, and children—passed through the fort.

At Fort Laramie, the travelers wrote letters to their families. They sent them back with fur traders who were heading east. Fort Laramie was less than half way to Oregon. From the fort, the Oregon Trail began winding up the **Rocky Mountains**.

Clothing

There was no place to buy clothes on the trail. Before they left home, **pioneer** women sewed clothing for the whole family. They brought needles and thread on the trip to mend torn pants and dresses.

DUST AND DIRT

Clothes were washed in water from the streams. They were hung on the wagons to dry. As the wagons rolled, dust stuck to the wet clothes, making them dirty all over again.

Clothes were washed and scrubbed by hand in tubs of water.

Women and girls had two or three dresses, a shawl, a bonnet, a scarf, an apron, and a couple of nightgowns. Men and boys had two or three pairs of pants, a few wool shirts, a scarf, and a hat or cap. Some men had jackets, too. Everyone wore strong leather boots or shoes.

NEW FOOTWEAR

Some pioneers got leather moccasins from the Native Americans. They found the moccasins to be quite comfortable.

When it got cold, travelers put on an extra layer of clothing.

Food

Pioneers carried dry foods such as rice, flour, beans, potatoes, and coffee. These would not **spoil** on the journey. Along the trail, men and children went fishing. Men also shot birds, deer, and sometimes buffalo. Women cooked the animal meat over a fire. Or, they added it to a pot of stew with onions and potatoes.

Most families cooked over a fire. Here is a typical menu:
BREAKFAST: coffee, bacon, bread or pancakes
LUNCH: cold, dried meat
DINNER: Bacon and beans or buffalo stew

Oregon Trail Recipe—Bacon Stew

Follow the instructions below to make a stew of bacon, beans, and rice as pioneers did in the 1850s. Pioneers started with dry red beans and cooked them in water for two hours. This recipe uses canned beans. It makes enough soup for four helpings.

WARNING: Do not cook anything unless there is an adult to help you. Always ask an adult to use knives, the stove, and to handle hot food.

YOU WILL NEED
1 cup (240 g) of rice
2 cups (480 ml) of water
1 small onion, cut up
2 tablespoons of oil
1/2 teaspoon salt
1/4 teaspoon garlic powder
dash of pepper
4 slices of bacon
1 16-ounce (32-gram) can of red beans

FOLLOW THE STEPS

1. Put 2 cups of water in a pan. Add 1/4 teaspoon of salt. Bring the water to a boil.
2. Add the rice to the boiling water. Lower the heat, and cover the pan with a lid. Cook for about 20 minutes until all the water is gone.

3. In another pan, heat the oil.
4. Cook the onions in the oil until the pieces are almost clear.
5. Pour the beans into a strainer and rinse them with water.
6. Mix the beans into the onions. Add the rest of the salt, pepper,

and garlic powder. Heat for 10 minutes.
7. Fry the bacon in a skillet until it is crisp.
8. Remove the bacon and break it into pieces. Mix the pieces with the beans.
9. Spoon the bean mixture over rice, mix together, and serve.

Oregon at Last

After many long months, the tired travelers finally reached Oregon. They were delighted to see **cabins** with smoke puffing from the chimneys. There were **crops** growing in fields. There were grown-ups working and children playing. These were the families who had arrived earlier.

On one of the last nights on the trail, people try to imagine their new life in Oregon.

The long trip was over. But there was much work to do. Families needed to build cabins and barns. They had to chop trees to clear a planting field. For the first few years, children were too busy to go to school.

The travelers arrive! Some had buried their parents and grandparents on the Oregon Trail. Some gave birth to new babies. All of them made friendships on the trail that would last the rest of their lives.

Oregon Grows

The travelers settled into the land. They built their houses and farms. Then they built schools, stores, and churches. Towns, such as Portland, Oregon, grew into large cities. Wagons rolled into Oregon through the 1880s. Thousands of wheels rolled over the Oregon Trail. Today you can still see the ruts they left in the dirt.

This busy town, set up by pioneers, has a hotel, bank, and many stores. In the 1850s, people began traveling west in **stagecoaches**.

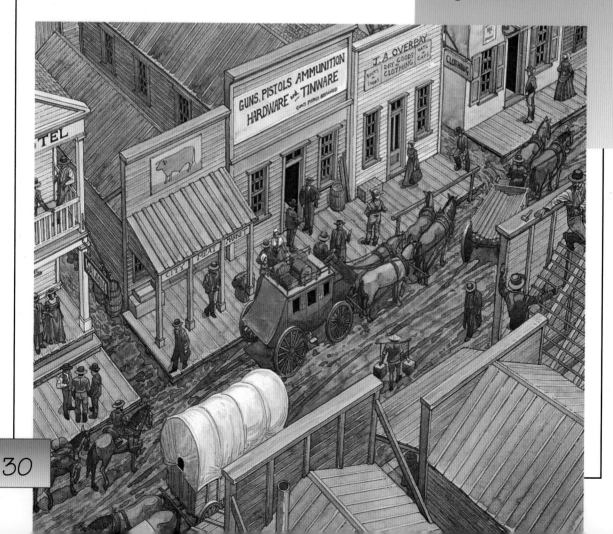

Glossary

cabin simple, small house, often built of logs

canvas thick material usually made from cotton

crops plants grown to provide food

fort strong building to protect people from attacks

fur trader person who exchanged objects or money for animal skins

guard someone who protects or keeps watch over people or a place

guide person who leads travelers on a journey or trip

oxen strong animals, related to cows, used to pull wagons or farm equipment

pioneer someone who does something or goes someplace first to make it easier for others to follow

plains wide area of flat or gently rolling land

prairie dog squirrel-like animal that digs and lives in underground tunnels

Rocky Mountains longest group of mountains in the U.S., stretching from Alaska to Mexico

slate writing surface used in schools, similar to a small blackboard

spoil to become rotten

stagecoach boxlike car pulled by horses that people rode in to travel long distances

trade to exchange one thing for another

wagon train group of covered wagons that traveled to the West together

---

More Books to Read

Loeper, John J. *Meet the Wards on the Oregon Trail.* Tarrytown, NY: Marshall Cavendish, 1999.

Stein, R. Conrad. *The Oregon Trail.* Danbury, Conn.: Children's Press, 1994.

Index